RHYTHM RHYMES

Chosen by

RUTH SANSOM

A. & C. BLACK : LONDON

PUBLISHED BY A. AND C. BLACK LTD

35 BEDFORD ROW, LONDON WCIR 4JH

FIRST EDITION 1964

REPRINTED 1969, 1974, 1975, 1976

© 1964 RUTH SANSOM

ISBN 0 7136 0681 9

PRINTED IN GREAT BRITAIN BY
TINDAL PRESS LIMITED
CHELMSFORD, ESSEX

CONTENTS

INTRODUCTION

These rhymes are meant to be spoken as an accompaniment to vigorous movement. Voice and action interpret the mood, pace and rhythm of the words.

This combination of rhyme and movement was first introduced to schools by the late Marjorie Gullan in her teaching and books.* As a former student and lecturer at the Speech Fellowship, I remember her with love and admiration, and have found that this type of work, for the reasons given below, is invaluable with young children:

It is the best possible preparation for the speaking of poetry

It helps children to appreciate rhythm by ' proving it upon their pulses '

They not only learn to listen with pleasure to the variety in phrase, pitch, pace and tone, but to experience it themselves

It helps to co-ordinate speech and movement

It helps to unify the child's personality, counteracting the division between thought and feeling that is a tendency in education. It can also have a stabilising influence on the emotionally unstable

These particular rhymes have been tested out in a number of schools in the last ten years by myself, and by Miss S. K. Vickery and others at the Speech Education Centre. My thanks go to them for many years of happy co-operation.

* *Poetry Speaking for Children*, Books 1–3, M. Gullan and P. Gurrey (Methuen).

I am also grateful to the following authors for permission to use copyright material :

Miss Evelyn Abraham for ' I walk on my toes ' and ' Upstairs, downstairs ' which first appeared in *Speech News*.

Miss Hilda Adams for ' Dance, dance ' and ' A long blue dragon ' from *Jingle Jangle* (A. & C. Black Ltd.).

Mrs Rodney Bennett for ' Chop chop ' from *First Steps in Speech Training* (Evans Bros. Ltd.).

Miss Mollie Clarke for ' Here I come lightly ' from *Raggle-Taggle Rhymes* (A. Wheaton & Co. Ltd.).

Mr Clive Sansom for verses from *Speech Rhymes* and *Acting Rhymes* (A. & C. Black Ltd.) and for others written especially for this book.

Miss S. K. Vickery, Mrs Marlene Lette, Miss Eleanor Spiegel, Miss Anne Kingston and Miss Elizabeth Morley for other rhymes first printed in this collection. Detailed acknowledgments are made in the index.

The rhymes have been arranged in three parts in order of difficulty. They range from the first Infant grade to top Primary, but their suitability depends largely on the class's previous experience. Suggestions on the use and speaking of the rhymes are given on page 69.

Rhythm rhymes, however, are only one aspect of speech education. Other activities such as creative drama, oral language games, group speaking and speech technique are fully described in *Speech and Communication in the Primary School* by Clive Sansom (A. & C. Black Ltd.).

R. S.

———

PART 1

WALKING WITH A TRAY

Hot cross buns,
Hot cross buns,
One a penny, two a penny,
Hot cross buns.

Hot cross buns,
Hot cross buns,
If you have no daughters,
Give them to your sons,
One a penny, two a penny,
Hot cross buns.

SKIPPING

Diddledy, diddledy, dumpty,
The cat ran up the plum tree.
Half a crown to fetch him down,
Diddledy, diddledy, dumpty.

(Repeat)

TIP-TOEING

Tippy tippy tippy tippy,
Tippy tippy tip-toe;
See the little hungry mice
Running in the snow, snow.

Tippy tippy tippy tippy,
Tippy tippy tip-toe;
They couldn't find a thing to eat
And so they had to go, go.

BOUNCING THE BALL

Bounce the ball, bounce the ball,
Bounce the ball high;
Bounce the ball, bounce the ball,
Let the ball die.

(Repeat)

GALLOPING

Gallop pony, gallop now,
Gallop, gallop, ho!
Gallop pony, gallop now,
Whoa! whoa! whoa!

(Repeat)

DRUMMING

Zinty tinty tuppenny bun,
The cook came out to have some fun.
He had some fun, he beat the drum,
Zinty tinty tuppenny bun.

HAMMERING AND SEWING

Rap-a-tap-a-tap-a-tap,
A-tick-a-tack-a-too!
A busy little hammer-man
Is mending up a shoe.
He sews the button on
With his teeny, tiny needle,
And, rap-a-tap-a-tap-a-tap,
A-tick-a-tack-a-teedle.

TIP-TOEING

Tip-toe, tip-toe,
That is how the pixies go;
Tip-toe, tip-toe,
Tripping lightly to and fro;
Tip-toe, tip-toe,
They can hear the daisies grow;
Tip-toe, tip-toe,
Softly come and softly go.

RIDING

(Slip step)

Bell horses, bell horses,
What time of day?
One o'clock, two o'clock,
Three and away.

(Repeat)

ROCKING

Sh! the baby's asleep now,
Sh! the baby's asleep;
Gently rock him, softly rock him,
Sh! the baby's asleep.
Sh! Sh!
Sh!

SKIPPING

If you can skip on the tips of your toes,
I'll give you a ribbon to tie into bows.
Skip! skip! for everyone knows
It's easy to skip on the tips of your toes.

ELEPHANT WALK

Plonk on this foot,
Plonk on that,
Swinging my trunk,
Swinging my trunk.
I'm out in the jungle
Without any hat,
Plonk on this,
Plonk on that!
I'll go to sleep
In the shade of a tree,
Nose on knee,
Nose on knee,
And no one will know
That it's only me.
Nod and nod,
Sleep and sleep.

PUSHING THE SWING

Swing me over the water,
Swing me over the sea,
Swing me over the garden wall,
And swing me home to tea.

ROCKING

Sleep, little boy,
Your father is fishing;
Sleep, little boy,
Your mother is wishing
That father would come
With a boat full of fish
And leave us with nothing
At all to wish.
Sleep, little boy,
Your father is fishing;
Sleep, little boy,
Your mother is wishing.

WALKING

Round and round the rose bush,
One step, two steps,
All the little girls and boys
Are sitting on the doorsteps.

(Repeat)

Clippety, cloppety,
Clippety, clop,
Hares will dance
And rabbits will hop;
Rabbits will hop
And lambs will skip
And bounce themselves
With a clippety clip.
Clip, clop,
Clippety clip!

TIP-TOEING

I'm tip-toeing here,
I'm tip-toeing there,
In my little blue slippers
I bought at the fair.
They tinkle and twinkle
Wherever I go,
The bells on my slippers
That swing to and fro.

PENDULUM SWINGING

The clock
Ticks,
The clock
Tocks,
This way,
That way,
And never, never
Stops.
Tick-tock
Tick-tock. . . .
    (*Fade*)

GALLOPING

Gallop aheigh! Gallop aheigh!
Christopher's pony is running away.
Gallop aheigh, he never will stay,
Christopher's pony has galloped away.
Galloped away,
Galloped away,
Christopher's pony has galloped away.

ROCKING

Sleep, my little new Teddy,
Tuck your head in my arm,
I'll hold you tight and I'll hold you warm,
You never will come to harm,
So sleep, my little new Teddy,
Tuck your head in my arm.

SKIPPING

Higglety, pigglety, pop,
The dog has eaten the mop;
The pig's in a hurry,
The cat's in a flurry,
Higglety, pigglety, pop!

ROCKING-HORSE

Rockety, rickety, rockety rick,
Here is my rocking-horse, rockety rick.
Rockety, rick, please be quick!
Rockety, rickety, rockety rick.

WALKING

Follow-my-leader, follow-my-leader,
Follow-my-leader, after me,
Follow me up to the top of the hill
And follow me down to the sea.

(*Repeat*)

TRAIN MOVEMENT

Chuffa-chuffa-chuffa-chuffa
I'm a noisy train,
Chuffa-chuffa-chuffa-chuffa
Steaming in the rain.

Chuff! chuff! chuff!
I'm putting on my brake!
Puff! puff! puff!
What a noise I make—
Who-o-o-o!

RIDING

This is the way the ladies ride,
Nim, nim, nim.

This is the way the gentlemen ride,
Trot, trot, trot.

And this is the way the hunters ride,
Gallop-aheigh, gallop-aheigh,
Gallop-aheigh, away, away.

HAMMERING

Tick tack too,
Mend a lady's shoe,
A red shoe, a red shoe,
Tick tack too.

Tick tack too,
Mend a giant's shoe,
A black shoe, a black shoe,
Tick tack too.

Tick tack too,
Mend a baby's shoe,
A white shoe, a white shoe,
Tick tack too.

Tick tack too,
Mend a horse's shoe,
An iron shoe, an iron shoe,
Tick tack too.

ROCKING

(*Hanging cradle*)

O little brown baby,
You're lying awake;
Hush-a-bye, hush,
It's growing so late:
The kittens are sleeping,
The puppies are too,
And soon I'll be sleeping—
Then what will you do?
So hush-a-bye, hush;
Close your eyes tight.
Stars will watch over you
All the long night.

WADDLING

See the little ducks come waddling down the lane,
  Waddle, waddle, quack!
  Waddle, waddle, quack!
Marching in the mud and paddling in the rain,
  Waddle, waddle, quack!
  Waddle, waddle, quack!
'We're going to the pond and we're never coming
   back again,'
  Waddle, waddle, quack, quack, quack!

TIP-TOEING

  Upstairs, downstairs,
  Creeping like a mouse,
  Creeping in the darkness
  Round and round the house.
  Creep, creep, creeping,
  Round and round about—
  I hope the wind won't come inside
  And blow my candle out.

RUNNING

Run round the sand-hills,
Chase after me.
Run to the water's edge
And paddle in the sea.

(Repeat)

DIGGING

I'm down on the beach
With my strong wooden spade,
Digging out the sand
Round the castle I have made.

(Repeat)

FROG JUMPING

Jump, froggie, jump,
Over the log with a ' glump!'
Stop for a rest,
Puff out your chest,
And jump, froggie, jump.

CHOPPING

Chop, chop,
Choppety, chop!
Chop off the bottom,
And chop off the top.
What there is left
We will pop in the pot;
Chop, chop,
Choppety, chop!

RIDING

To horse, my good master,
At break of the day,
A canter, a canter,
Then gallop away.

Gallop away,
Gallop away,
A canter, a canter,
Then gallop away.

WALKING

When the rain falls fast
Or the rain falls slow,
The postman with his load
Goes walking up the road.
On his back a mackintosh,
On his head a cap,
Stopping at the door
With a rap, tap-tap.

TIP-TOEING

I walk on my toes,
I walk on my toes;
Where I am going to
Nobody knows.
Nobody knows,
But all the way
I'll walk on my toes
The whole of the day!

23

DRUMMING

Rumpety-tum
On the drum, drum,
Listen. . . .
Listen. . . .
Rumpety-tum
On the drum, drum,
Rumpety-tumpety-tum.

WALKING

(Chickens)

Hickety, pickety,
   My black hen,
She lays eggs
   For gentlemen;
Sometimes nine,
   And sometimes ten.
Hickety, pickety,
   My black hen!

DANCING

Dancing, dancing,
There she goes,
Little Miss Prue
On pretty pink toes;
Tippety—tippety
Trippety—trippety
Skippety—skippety skip.

STIRRING

(Quick stir)

Porridge is bubbling,
Bubbling hot,
Stir it round
And round in the pot.
The bubbles plip!
The bubbles plop!
It's ready to eat
All bubbling hot.

DANCING

Dance, little fairy,
Dance and sing;
Lightfoot and airy
Dance in the ring.

Sit, little fairy,
Fold your wings:
Wait for the gift
That the goblin brings.

CARPET-BEATING

Beat the carpet,
Beat the carpet,
Swish! Swish!

The dust flies—
Shut your eyes.
Swish! Swish!

WING FLAPPING

Cock-a-doodle doo—
Peter has lost his shoe,
Meg has lost her pencil box
And doesn't know what to do—
Cock-a-doodle doo—
A hulla-balloo-balloo—

TROTTING

Trot, trot, trot, trot,
Softly in the snow,
Pad, pad, pad, pad,
See the huskies go.

☃

PART 2

WALKING WITH A SWING

Follow my Bangalorey man,
Follow my Bangalorey man;
I'll do all that ever I can
To follow my Bangalorey man.

(Repeat)

SKIPPING

Tom, Tom, the piper's son,
Learned to play when he was young,
But the only tune that he could play
Was 'Over the hills and far away'.
Far away, far away,
Over the hills and far away.

CHURNING

Come, butter, come,
Come, butter, come.
Peter's standing at the gate
Waiting for a buttered cake—
Come, butter, come,
Come, butter, come.

Come, butter, come,
Come, butter, come.
Mary's standing at the gate
Waiting for a buttered cake—
Come, butter, come,
Come, butter, come.

GALLOPING

Gee up, gee up, and gallop away,
Gee up, my piebald pony.
The day is short, the way is long,
The road is rough and stony.

Into the dark, I gallop away,
Over the heath in a hurry—
A highwayman with a coach to meet,
Away in the woods of Surrey.

TIP-TOEING

Tip . . . toe,
Soft and slow,
Under the willow trees,
Over the snow,
Bells are ringing;
To church we'll go,
Tip . . . toe
Over the snow.

RUNNING

Run, run, run,
Have a little fun,
In and out the shadows
And in and out the sun.
In and out the sun,
And in and out the rain,
Running in our bare feet
Down the leafy lane.

CHINESE HURRY-WALK

Ting-a-ling, ting-a-ling,
Bing, bang, bong.
What a lot of Chinamen
Hurrying along.
Hurry up, hurry up,
Run, run, run,
All the way to Chinaland,
Oh what fun!

WINDSCREEN WIPER

Flicker flicker flack!
Flicker flicker flack!
The wiper on the car goes
Flicker flicker flack,
The rain falls flick!
And the rain falls flack!
And the wiper on the car goes
Flicker, flicker, flack!
Flick!
Flack!

STALKING

A long file of Indians
Is creeping through the wood,
Walking in their moccasins
As every Indian should.
Quiet stand the trees;
Still waits the bear;
Soon there comes an arrow
Singing through the air—
      PING!

SKIPPING

We're skipping along for pleasure and fun,
Not minding the wind, or the rain, or the sun.

Our pockets with pennies go jingle and jangle,
And skip all about in a tingle and tangle.

MARCHING

Oh, the grand old Duke of York,
He had ten thousand men;
He marched them up to the top of the hill
And he marched them down again.

And when they were up, they were up,
And when they were down, they were down;
And when they were only halfway up
They were neither up nor down!

ROCKING-HORSE

To Cathay, to Cathay,
On my little horse of grey:
  Hey, hey, hey!
Away, my little pony!

To Japan, to Japan,
On my little horse of tan:
  Hey, hey, hey!
Away, my little pony!

To Peru, to Peru,
On my little horse of blue:
  Hey, hey, hey!
Away, my little pony!

All the night, all the night,
On my little horse of white:
  Hey, hey, hey!
Away, my little pony!

Coming back, coming back,
On my little horse of black:
  Hey, hey, hey!
Whoa, my little pony!

CLIMBING

Climbing up the hillside
Beneath the shady trees;
Legs are weary, backs are weary
Lifting up our knees.

Sit and rest your aching back,
Lean against a tree.
Look across the valley—
And tell me what you see.

ROCKING

Sleep, baby, sleep!
Thy father watches the sheep,
Thy mother is shaking the dreamland tree
And softly a little dream falls on thee,
Sleep, baby, sleep!

DRUMMING

Marching through the street
Come the drummers as they beat
The big bass drum—
Rum, tum, tum!

Walking with a stride,
The children march beside
The big bass drum—
Rum, tum, tum!

Swinging arms along,
Marching with a song,
Rum, tum, tum!
The big bass drum—
Rum, rum,
Rum, tum, tum!

DANCING

Oh, I kick up my heels
And dance a jig,
And nobody cares
If I'm little or big.

Nobody cares
If I'm short or tall
Or whether I'm round
Like a bouncing ball.
Fiddle-di-dee,
Twiddle-di-dee,
Kick up your heels
And dance with me.

HAMMERING

Hammering here,
Hammering there,
Hammering nails
To make you a chair.
Nails are straight,
Hammer is true,
Hit every head
As the workmen do :—
Whack !
Whack !

GOBLINS WALKING

Goblins, little goblins,
They are creeping on their toes
Down the fairy meadows
Where the magic mushroom grows,
Searching for a rabbit
With an itchy-twitchy nose.

Faster, little goblins,
Faster you must tread
In your little shoes of green
And your little coats of red,
Or the itchy-twitchy rabbit
Will have run away to bed.

ROWING

Row, boys, row,
As up the river we go,
With a long pull
And a strong pull
Row, boys, row.

(Repeat)

RUNNING

Tip-tap, tip-tap,
Tip-tap-tee,
Here comes a little man
Running on the lea.
Tip-tap, tip-tap,
He can't catch me,
I'm hiding in the branches
Of the old oak tree.

STIRRING CAULDRON

Binx, minx, the old Witch winks,
The fat begins to fry;
There's no one at home but Jumping Joan,
The old black cat, and I.

Binx, minx, the old Witch winks,
The fish jump out of the pan;
Jumping Joan is off to the moon
As fast as ever she can.

ELEPHANT WALKING

We're swaying through the jungle
Dizzy with the heat,
Searching for a water-hole
To cool our heavy feet.

Trample on the grasses;
Then stop and breathe the scent
Of flower and leaf—and tiger!
And we watch the way he went.

Then on again we stumble,
Searching for a drink;
We find a spilling river,
And into it we sink.

DRUMMING

Tum-tumpty-tum,
The cat is playing the drum;
Four little mice are shaking the ground,
Dancing merrily round and round,
Tum-tumpty-tum.

Tum-tumpty-tum,
The cat is playing the drum;
Three little mice are shaking the ground
Dancing merrily round and round,
Tum-tumpty-tum.

Tum-tumpty-tum,
The cat is playing the drum;
Two little mice are shaking the ground,
Dancing merrily round and round,
Tum-tumpty-tum.

Tum-tumpty-tum,
The cat is playing the drum;
One little mouse is shaking the ground,
Dancing merrily round and round,
Tum-tumpty-tum.

WALKING IN PAIRS

Darby and Joan are dressed in black,
Sword and buckle behind their back.
One by one, and two by two,
Turn about quickly, and that will do.

CRADLE ROCKING

Hush-a-bye baby, lie still, lie still,
Your mother has gone to the mill, the mill.
Baby's not sleeping for want of good keeping,
Hush-a-bye baby, lie still, lie still.

WALKING

Twiddle-di-dee, twiddle-di-dee,
I went for a walk with a bumble bee,
Past the farm and the linden tree;
Buzz, buzz, twiddle-di-dee!

TREE-CHOPPING

Chop and chip,
Chop and chip,
Cut down a tree
To build your ship.

Chip and chop,
Chip and chop,
Wait for the call
That tells you to stop.
Chip, chop, chip, chop,
Chip, chop. . . .

TIMBER !

SAWING WOOD

See-saw, saw the wood,
Saw it through and through,
Down and up, down and up,
Till the wood is cut in two.
Zz—Zz
Zz—Zz
Zz—Zz—Zz.

GOING TO THE SEA
(*Changing rhythms*)

Walk :   Walking in my red shoes,
Down the busy street,
Walking in my red shoes,
Whom do you think we'll meet?
'Hullo, Jane.' (*Children greet a friend*)

Tramp :   Tramping in my black shoes,
Down the muddy lane,
Tramping in my black shoes
Through the dripping rain.

Skip :   Skipping on my bare toes
Beside the sandy sea,
Up the beach and back again,
Up the beach and back again
And into the rolling sea.

Swimming   I swim—and I swim,
movement : On the billows—I ride,
I float—and I float
With the swing of the tide.

44

Skip :   Then out of the sea,
            And on to the sand,
            I skippety-skip
            To the beat of the band
            And away from the rolling sea.

STIRRING

(Slow stir)

A stir for me,
And a stir for you,
A stir for the cat,
And the baby too.
Put in a sixpence
Just for luck,
Put in a horse-shoe
And cover it up.
Christmas is coming,
The presents are done,
Stir up the pudding
And then for the fun.

BELL-RINGING

Ding, ding-a-dong,
Ding, ding-a-dong,
Ding-dong, ding-dong,
Ding-dong—
The bells in the steeple
Call to the people
Come, do come,
A wedding's begun.
Ding, ding-a-dong,
Ding, ding-a-dong,
Ding-dong, ding-dong,
Ding-dong—

SWINGING

When I swing on my swing
The birds all sing,
The flowers all sway,
The children play.
And oh! how happy
And oh! how gay
To swing on my swing
In the heat of the day.

SKIPPING

Jack in the Green
Went to play
Over the grass
In Bantry Bay.
After his shadow
He danced away
And didn't come back
Till Michaelmas day.

SWINGING

Swing me low,
Swing me high,
Over the grasses
As high as the sky.
Hair flying out,
Wind rushing by,
Like birds in the blue
We swing and we fly,
Higher . . .
Fly . . .

MARCHING

Rappetty-tappetty, teetlety-tootlety,
Oh what a wonderful noise!
Down the street with a teetlety-tootlety
Follow the girls and boys.
Teetlety-tootlety,
Teetlety-tootlety,
Teetlety-tootlety,
Toot!

RUNNING

On his two brown feet
The gingerbread man
Goes running down the street:
Catch him if you can.

The cook runs fast,
Behind the little man,
And her daughter runs last
With a pancake in a pan.

So run, run, run,
With the gingerbread man.

SKIPPING LIGHTLY

Fairies are dancing
In moonlit rings,
Skipping along
In their silver wings;
With never a thought,
Never a care,
Fairies are frolicking
Everywhere.

SPINNING

Spin—spin—
Big red top,
Spin on the floor
With a hip and a hop.

With a hip, and a hop,
And a hip—hip—hop,
Spin on the floor,
Big red top.

GALLOPING

(Smooth gallop)

Follow your husky over the track,
Follow him there and follow him back.
The sled is hissing and hissing along,
The wolves are howling a hungry song.
Follow your husky, never look back,
Follow him, follow him, over the track.

SPINNING WHEEL

Spin. . . . Spin. . . .
My little humming wheel,
Hoidi—oidi—oidi,
Hoidi—oidi—oidi.

Hum. . . . Hum. . . .
My little spinning wheel,
Hoidi—oidi—oidi,
The gold is falling gently.
Spin. . . . Spin. . . .
Hum. . . . Hum. . . .

PART 3

DWARFS WALKING

TRAMP-tramp, TRAMP-tramp,
TRAMP-tramp, TRAMP—
Every little digger-dwarf
Is holding up his lamp.

Sleepy . . . and Sneezy,
Dopey . . . and Doc,
All marching home again
At five by the clock.

Happy . . . and Grumpy,
Bashful . . . and me,
All the little digger-dwarfs
Coming back to tea.

TRAMP-tramp, TRAMP-tramp,
TRAMP-tramp, TRAMP—
Every little digger-dwarf
Is holding up his lamp.

SKIPPING

Hicketty picketty, pizer jiggitty,
Pompalorum jig :
Every man that has no hair
He ought to wear a wig.
A sixpenny bit on the tuppenny railway,
Half a crown on the rollicking sea,
And nothing at all on the hurdy-gurdy—
That's the one for me !

PAINTING

Have you been out painting,
Helping father with the fence ?
   Splish, splash, splosh !
   Splish, splash, splosh !

Stretching up and stretching down,
Painting every paling brown,
   Splish, splash, splosh !
   Splish, splash, splosh !

CANOEING

Dip your paddle
And pull with a will,
The river is sleepy,
And quiet, and still;
The blade cuts deep,
Ripples spread wide,
Rest on your paddle
And drift with the tide.

RUNNING

Yellow dog dingo
Runs down the track,
All the other yellow dogs
Running at his back.

Looking for their dinner,
Searching in a pack,
Yellow dog dingoes
Running down the track.

BOAT-HAULING

Hey, dor-a-lot, dor-a-lot,
Hey, dor-a-ley, dor-a-ley,
Hey, my bonny boat, bonny boat,
Hey, drag away, drag away.

STRONG ROPE-HAULING

Blow the man down, bullies, blow the man down;
  Wey, hey, blow the man down.
Blow the man down, bullies, blow him right down:
  Give us a chance to blow the man down.

Blow him right down from the top of his crown;
  Wey, hey, blow the man down.
Blow him right down from the top of his crown,
  Give us a chance to blow the man down!

SLOW WALKING

The noise that annoys
All the naughty little boys
Is the tramp of the feet
Of the Policeman on his beat,
As he walks up and down
With a frown, with a frown,
As he walks up and down with a frown.

When he holds up his hand
All the traffic has to stand;
Every car, every bus,
Has to stop without a fuss.
They must wait in a row
Till the Policeman tells them, 'Go!'
They must wait till the Policeman tells them, 'Go!'

And if anyone's about
Who shouldn't be about,
Then there isn't any doubt
He must very soon look out
For the tramp of the feet
Of the Policeman on his beat,
For the tramp of his feet on the beat.

DANCING A JIG

Strike up a jig on your fiddle, Maloney,
Strike up a jig on your bow.
We'll trip it and dance,
And kick it and prance
Till the mountains are white in the moon,
    so—
Strike up a jig on your fiddle, Maloney,
Strike up a jig on your bow.

HAMMERING

Clang goes the hammer
As we crack every rock,
While the clock in the steeple
Says—tick-tock!
For roads must be cut
With a whack and a wham,
So fill every rut
And ram, ram, ram!

LIGHT ROCKING

Gently, gently,
Swing in your cradle,
Little brown coon
In your fine plaited cradle.
No bear from the forest
Can find you nor take you,
No lion, no tiger,
No bear from the forest.
So gently, gently,
Swing in your cradle,
Little brown coon
In your fine plaited bed.

TURNING HANDLE

Turn, cheeses, turn,
Turn, cheeses, turn,
Green cheeses, yellow laces,
Up and down the market places.
Turn, cheeses, turn,
Turn, cheeses, turn.

HAULING LIGHT ROPE

A handy ship and a handy crew,
   Handy, my boys, so handy;
A handy ship and a handy crew,
   Handy, my boys, away O!

A handy skipper and a second mate too,
   Handy, my boys, so handy;
A handy skipper and a second mate too,
   Handy, my boys, away O!

A handy bosun and a handy chips,
   Handy, my boys, so handy;
A handy bosun and a handy chips,
   Handy, my boys, away O!

ROPE-HAULING

There's a black ball Barque coming down the
   river—
   Blow, bullies, blow!
Her masts and yards they shine like silver,
   Blow, my bully-boys, blow!

Oh, blow, my boys, and blow for ever,
  Blow, bullies, blow!
And blow her home to the London river,
  Blow, my bully-boys, blow!

ROPE-HAULING

Away, haul away, boys; haul away together,
  Away, haul away, boys; haul away O!
Away, haul away, boys; haul away together,
  Away, haul away, boys; haul away O!

Louis was the King of France before the
    Revolution,
  Away, haul away, boys; haul away O!
Louis was the King of France before the
    Revolution,
  Away, haul away, boys; haul away O!

But Louis got his head cut off, and spoilt his
    Constitution,
  Away, haul away, boys; haul away O!
Louis got his head cut off, and spoilt his
    Constitution,
  Away, haul away, boys; haul away O!

CRADLE ROCKING

Little one, hush!
Tiny one, hush!
Birds with their singing
Set the hills ringing:
Blackbird and thrush,
Blackbird and thrush.

Little one, sleep!
Tiny one, sleep!
In the green meadows,
Cropping their shadows,
Graze the white sheep,
Graze the white sheep.

Little one, dream!
Tiny one, dream!
Bright swans are sailing,
Lazily sailing,
Down on the stream,
Down on the stream.

GOLLIWOG WALK

Golliwogs are walking
With their straight black legs.
They're black as night, their eyes are white,
They look like wooden pegs.
They stump along with elbows stiff,
And heads held high,
Staring straight in front of them,
As they go walking by.

Golliwogs are drooping,
Drooping with the heat,
They've lost their spring, they've not a thing
To keep them stiff and neat.
They flop along as limp as string,
Their heads are drooping low,
The floor is rising up to them—
They've all . . . let . . . go.

TROTTING

Clip-clop, clip-clop, clip-clop—
Hear the dog-cart trot down the lane;
Clip-clop to the town, and clop home again,
Clip-clop, clip-clop, clip-clop!

THE WITCHES' RIDE

The witches are galloping into the night,
Riding high on their brooms.
They're racketting down the milky way,
Between the stars and moons.
They're gliding over the chimneys now,
Streaming under the trees,
They're toppling down like a thunder shower,
Their cloaks spread out in the breeze.

PENDULUM SWINGING

Grandfather clock,
Grandfather clock,
Do you never stop tick,
And never stop tock ?
Tick ! Tock !
Tick ! Tock !
Never shall I stop
My tick and tock,
Tick ! Tock !
Tick ! Tock !
Dong ! Dong !
Dong !
Three o'clock.

WALKING UNDER SEA

I'm walking the bed of the ocean,
Exploring under the sea,
Pushing against the current,
Lifting arm and knee.

I lean my weight on the water,
And look between the weed,
Then through the shafts of sunlight
I watch the fishes feed.

DANCING

Dance . . . dance . . .
Dance around the lavender bush !
Dance . . . dance . . .
Under the mulberry tree !
  Dance with Jenny
  And dance with Jill,
  Dance with Bobby
  And dance with Bill,
Dance with anyone else you will—
But please dance with me !

LASSOO SWINGING

I'm swinging around my long lassoo,
Swing, swing, swirl!

I'm swinging around my long lassoo,
Swing, swing—hurl!

Hold it!
   Pull!

MARCHING

(*Knees up*)

I want to march. . . .
   I want to march. . . .
      I want to march
         Right down
            That street.

I want to skip. . . .
   I want to skip. . . .
      I want to skip
         Right down
            That street.

GALLOPING

Following fast,
Following fast,
See the Red Indian
Galloping past!

He's over the wagon,
He's over the brook,
He's into the camp
And he's frightened the cook.

Following fast,
Following fast,
See the Red Indian
Galloping past!

THE CAT'S DANCE

A cat came fiddling out of a barn
With a pair of bagpipes under her arm;
She could sing nothing but 'Fiddle-de-dee,
The mouse has married the bumble bee.'
Pipe, cat; dance, mouse;
We'll have a wedding at our good house.

WALKING LIGHTLY

Here I come lightly
Over the heather;
Little green pixie,
Little red feather.
Blow away wind and
Blow away feather,
Fly away, pixie,
Over the heather.

BELL-RINGING

Bells on the hilltop
Are ringing their chime,
'Dingledong! dongledong!
Tell us the time.'

'Time for all children
To start on their climb,
And (Dingledong! dongledong!)
Come here in time.'

STRIDING

Here comes a giant in his seven-league boots;
A great big fellow with black curly hair.
See him stride, and sway, and swagger,
Watch him swing his club through the air.
Now he's climbing up the great hillside,
Look how his legs span rivers and trees.
We couldn't catch him even on horseback,
He would escape us by leaping the seas.

ROPE SKIPPING

Salt and pepper,
Vinegar, mustard,
Cinnamon, cloves
And spice;
Over our heads
With a twirly whirly,
Apples and pears
And rice.

CREEPING

A long blue dragon
  Is creeping through the village.
He's lashing his tail,
  And he's tossing his head.
Run, little children,
  Run into your houses;
Run into your houses,
  And jump into bed! . . .

CATERPILLAR WALK

High on a leaf,
As happy as could be,
There sat a little caterpillar
Nibbling at a tree.

He went for a walk
With his one, two, three,
A fat little caterpillar
Creeping on a tree.

It is important to remember that these rhymes are not merely to give children an excuse for movement. *They are intended to synchronise exactly with the movement.* Speech and action should both express the rhythm of the words.

The word ' rhythm ', however, needs to be interpreted freely, and not to be confused with the mechanical repetition of metre.

This means that the teacher's voice should be flexible. It should have a wide range of pitch, and be capable of varying in tone, pace and energy. The teacher who finds this difficult at first needs to practise so that she gradually learns to give more variety, making her voice respond to the different idea and mood of each rhyme. This is essential, because if the speaking is not varied and flexible, the movement cannot be.

With some of the rhymes it is necessary to give full value to the rhythmic pause (or ' silent beat ') which occurs at the end of some lines, in order to make up the even number of stresses for the particular verse form, e.g. ' Marching ' :

The grand old Duke of York,

He had ten thousand men ;

He marched them up to the top of the hill

And he marched them down again

The movement continues even when the voice is silent.

Give the children as much space as possible. Where a hall or activity-room is available, they can all move at the same time. In the classroom, chairs and tables may be put either to the centre or the sides. Where this is not possible, the children may form lines in the aisles ; provided that one aisle is left free and the children can move round the back of the classroom, the activities can go on indefinitely. A nod from the teacher as she begins to speak a rhyme is enough to bring a row of children round the front, up the empty aisle, along the back, and down to their original places.

Children respond easily to the teacher's suggestion that a rhyme may make them want to walk, dance, gallop or move in some other way. We need not say specifically what that movement is.

When a number of rhymes have been introduced in this way, they may be spoken one after another, the children listening intently and changing their movement according to the activity and mood suggested.

There comes a time when some of the children will wish to help the teacher with the speaking. This may be encouraged in the less vigorous rhymes such as rocking, creeping and walking. But with more vigorous movement (e.g. marching, running, galloping) a small separate speaking-group is advisable : otherwise the speaking becomes breathless and jerky. This development should not be forced, yet children do find an added enjoyment in matching the speech with the movement.

Children should be encouraged to move lightly in bare feet or soft shoes. If they cannot hear the words, they cannot interpret them and the value of the lesson is lost.

There may be times when the teacher finds it necessary to work with the children either sitting in their desks or standing beside them. Several rhymes lend themselves to this situation. The ' tick-tock ' of a pendulum, hammering, beating the carpet, stirring and chopping need vigorous movement on the spot. Action should be as free and varied as possible, so long as the rhythm is kept.

Walking

Each of these is different in pace and mood. Children should be encouraged to listen carefully and show these differences in the way they walk. The natural stressing of the words indicates the rhythm :

> I walk on my toes,
>
> I walk on my toes ;
>
> Where I am going to
>
> Nobody knows

In some of the rhymes there is a change of movement leading to stillness, e.g. 'Elephant Walk' :

Plonk on this foot,	I'll go to sleep
Plonk on that,	In the shade of a tree,
Swinging my trunk,	Nose on knee,
Swinging my trunk.	Nose on knee. . . .

Skipping and dancing

Encourage variety of movement. The children will adapt their steps to a quick, light tone of voice :

> If you can skip on the tips of your toes

or a slower, more vigorous type :

> Higglety, pigglety, pop,
>
> The dog has eaten the mop

even improvising simple dances to :

> Oh, I kick up my heels
>
> And dance a jig

so long as word and movement continue to coincide.

71

Swinging

In the following rhyme :

> Swing me over the water,
>
> Swing me over the sea

the natural sense-rhythm gives one strong stress at the beginning of each line for the push of the swing, and the rest of the line for recovery after the movement forward. If we make two forward pushes in the line, we are bound to distort the word ' water ' by giving emphasis to the unstressed syllable ' er '.

Galloping, Riding, Trotting

Each rhyme suggests a slightly different movement.

> Gallop pony, gallop now

is more controlled than :

> Gallop a-heigh

whereas

> Bell horses, bell horses,   What time of day

is so fast that it turns into a sideways slip-step.

A precise trotting movement, with knees well lifted in front, is needed for :

> Clip-clop, clip-clop, clip-clop
>
> Hear the dog-cart trot down the lane ;
>
> Clip-clop to the town and clop home again,
>
> Clip-clop, clip-clop, clip-clop

Rocking-horse

' To Cathay ' is most successful when stressed as follows, with one main emphasis to each line :

72

To Cathay, to Cathay,

On my little horse of grey ;

Hey, hey, hey !

Away, my little pony

Rock forward on the stressed word and recover on the rest of the line.

Rocking

The children invent a number of different actions for rocking but come to grief if the rhythm is not clearly heard in the speaker's voice. Some may stand and rock backwards and forwards, or from side to side, some walk with a pram, some rock a cradle, and others rock with their knees on the floor.

Sometimes there is one stress (i.e. one push) to the line and a recovery on the unstressed syllables. Sometimes there are two stresses or pushes in the line :

(i) Sh, the baby's asleep now,

Sh, the baby's asleep

(ii) O little brown baby,

You're lying awake

(iii) Hush-a-bye baby, lie still, lie still,

Your mother has gone to the mill, the mill

Hammering

The words suggest different kinds of hammers : very small, medium or a large rock-breaking hammer that swings with its own weight :

Rap-a-tap-a-tap-a-tap

73

suggests small movement ;

> Tick tack too,
>
> Mend a lady's shoe

suggests larger movement ; and the road-menders swing from the hips :

> Clang goes the hammer
>
> As we crack every rock

Frog-jump

> Jump, froggie, jump,
>
> Over the log with a ' glump '

The children rest during the next two lines, and finish up with two jumps.

Running

A controlled run is possible when children bring their feet well up at the back :

> Run round the sand-hills,
>
> Chase after me

> Tip-tap, tip-tap,
>
> Tip-tap-tee

Tracking

An opportunity for subtle timing occurs in the rhyme :

> A long file of Indians (*step*)
>
> Is creeping through the wood (*step*),
>
> Walking in their moccasins (*step*)
>
> As every Indian should (*step*)

The last two syllables of the words 'Indians' and 'moccasins' should not be stressed, but spoken naturally. During the rest of the rhyme the children may want to stand still and prepare the bow and arrow.

Beating Carpet
Vigorous speech encourages vigorous action :

> Beat the carpet,
>
> <u>Swish</u> !
>
> Beat the carpet,
>
> <u>Swish</u> !   (*Beat—recover*)

Tip-Toeing
Follow the natural sense-stress with four stresses (steps) to each line in

> Tippy tippy tippy tippy,
>
> Tippy tippy tip-toe

Occasionally there is a rhyme such as

> Upstairs, downstairs,
>
> Creeping like a mouse

which may be given four stresses in the line, or two stresses :

> Upstairs, downstairs,
>
> Creeping like a mouse

without distorting the speech. But definitely two stresses only to each line in :

> I'm tip-toeing here,
>
> I'm tip-toeing there,
>
> In my little blue slippers

INDEX

The rhymes are arranged alphabetically according to activity